Original title:
Peppermint Wishes and Mistletoe Dreams

Copyright © 2024 Creative Arts Management OÜ
All rights reserved.

Author: Tobias Winslow
ISBN HARDBACK: 978-9916-94-080-8
ISBN PAPERBACK: 978-9916-94-081-5

The Warm Embrace of Tradition

In a cozy home, the lights twinkle bright,
A cat on the table, a curious sight.
Granny's fruitcake sits, a mystery to unfold,
We take cautious bites, it's a taste to behold.

Children in pajamas, they dance and they prance,
Wearing reindeer antlers, they giggle and glance.
Mom's secret eggnog, it's a festive delight,
But last year's batch gave Dad quite the fright.

Uncle Joe tells tales, they seem far too tall,
About the one time he bowled with a wall.
Grandpa's snoring loud, a merry, soft tune,
While pie in the oven sets a sweet mood soon.

Outside, snowflakes swirl, kids bundled up tight,
Snowmen with hats that are slightly too bright.
Tradition's embrace, it wraps us with cheer,
In this warm, quirky chaos, we hold dear.

Sweets of December and Warm Embrace

Gingerbread men dance with flair,
Sugarplum pixies twirl in the air.
Hot cocoa spills from a wayward cup,
As marshmallows bounce and pop right up.

Snowflakes tumble with a silly grin,
Warming mittens hiding mischief within.
Laughter bubbles in each frosty cheer,
While cookie crumbs whisper tales in the rear.

Nocturnal Serenades and Fairy Lights

Elves in pajamas sing out with glee,
Singing silly songs by the old pine tree.
Tinsel twinkles as cats pounce and chase,
Under fairy lights, they dash with grace.

The moon winks down at the frosty scene,
While shadows of snowmen look rather mean.
A snowdog barks at a passing sleigh,
As giggles erupt, come join in the play!

Wishes in a Snowglobe

Inside a globe, a world spins slow,
Penguins that dance, putting on a show.
A snowman tips his hat with flair,
While the polar bear jumps in mid-air.

Wishes swirl in a lazy whirl,
Candy canes sprout like an unexpected pearl.
Giggles erupt from the frozen scene,
As wishes fly high, bold and keen!

Hushed Carols and Fragrant Fires

Under the stars, a choir sings low,
While sugar plums wiggle with joy, oh!
Cinnamon swirls fill the crisp night air,
As the dog tries to join in, with flair.

Crackling wood sings to the sage and thyme,
With each silly note, it must be prime time.
Dress up the cat for a grand holiday,
Impress the guests in a furry display!

Twinkling Moments

When the lights go out, we dance with glee,
A cat on the tree, oh what a sight to see!
Cookies are baking, but who's to blame?
The dog just jumped high, playing his game.

Tinsel in a tangle, it clings like glue,
Grandma is laughing, wearing her shoe!
We raise a toast with cocoa and cheer,
For all the silly stories that keep us near.

Soft Elves and Twinkling Lights

Elves in the corner, plotting their flair,
Wrapping up gifts, but losing a pair!
Socks that don't match, a glorious mess,
Yet every oddity, we love no less.

With twinkling lights and laughter so bright,
We'll dance like fools, oh what a delight!
A snowball fight breaks out in the hall,
Who knew holiday spirit could lead to a brawl?

Cherished Memories in Every Flake

As snowflakes fall, we jump and scream,
They're soft as a pillow; it feels like a dream!
Fingers are freezing, noses all red,
Hot cider awaits us, a joy to be fed.

We gather 'round stories of years gone by,
Of clumsy old Santa, oh my, oh my!
With laughter erupting, we hold back the tears,
Each moment we cherish, through all of the years.

The Essence of Yule

A funny hat worn by Uncle Joe,
He swears it's stylish, but we just go slow!
Chickens do cluck as they flutter and run,
While pies on the table may not be well done.

Candles are flickering, but not quite aligned,
As Grandma reads fortunes, we just laugh combined.
With smiles and giggles, we raise our good cheer,
For nothing's more joyful than friends gathered near.

Stars that Show the Way

Twinkling lights in the sky,
Show me where I should fly.
I tripped on a snowflake, oh no!
My hot cocoa has put on a show.

With a wink and a nod from above,
I danced like a silly little dove.
The stars giggle, shining bright,
While I slip and slide with delight.

Tinsel and Tales

Tinsel hangs like a shimmery clown,
While I wear my best Christmas gown.
The cat starts to climb the tree,
And knocks over my cup of tea.

Old tales spun by firelight,
Of reindeer that took off in flight.
But who knew they'd be so loud?
As they jumped and danced, I laughed out loud.

The Allure of Winter Nights

Winter nights are full of flair,
With snowflakes falling everywhere.
A snowball fight turns into a war,
And somehow, I've lost my galore.

Hot chocolate spills, it's a sticky mess,
My tongue's stuck out—it's a real stress!
But laughter bounces off the trees,
As we catch snowflakes on our knees.

Brightly Colored Fantasies

Bright colors dance in every cheer,
While my holiday hat flops in the rear.
I juggle ornaments, what a sight,
As my dog thinks it's time for a bite.

Candy canes stuck in my hair,
Gingerbread men running everywhere.
We laugh till we drop, it's pure delight,
In this crazy, festive night!

Aromas of Joy and Cheer

The cookies are burning, oh what a sight,
A batch done gone wrong on this chilly night.
The cocoa is spilled all over the floor,
But laughter erupts, who could ask for more?

The tree is uneven, it leans to the side,
Ornaments dropping, no place left to hide.
Tinsel and ribbons, a colorful show,
With a cat on the prowl, what could go wrong though?

The Spirit of the Season

A turkey that dances, we swear that it's true,
It jiggles and wiggles, just like me and you.
We toast with hot cider, all raise up a cheer,
And find out our glasses were filled with warm beer!

The stockings are hung with mischief and glee,
Did Aunt Edna stuff hers with pickles for me?
While carols are sung in an off-key parade,
We think 'tis the season for joyful charades!

Twinkling Lights and Tender Moments

String lights around houses, oh what a feat,
But tangled in wires, we can't find our feet.
A ladder that wobbles, a clip that goes snap,
We laugh at the trouble, and then take a nap.

The snowflakes are falling, quite sudden and fast,
The kids are all running, they hope it'll last.
We build up a snowman, with carrots for eyes,
And wait for him to sneeze—oh, what a surprise!

Merriment in the Snow

A snowball fight breaks out, oh what a blast,
With mittens gone missing, we'll surely be last.
We sail down the hill on a sled that won't steer,
But giggles abound, and we find winter dear.

Then hot soup is served, but it's way too hot,
With marshmallows floating, we'll sip what we've got.
As laughter rings out, and the night starts to fade,
We wriggle with joy, each moment well played.

Hopes Strung Around the Tree

Colorful lights twinkle bright,
As uncle Bob starts a food fight.
Grandma's cookies, slightly burnt,
Santa's sleigh? It's just a skirt.

The cat's climbed high, oh what a scene,
Knocking down ornaments, so mean!
Kids in PJs, sugar-fueled,
They're laughing hard, they'll never be schooled.

Tinsel flutters, oh, how it gleams,
Caught in the attic's forgotten dreams.
Jingle bells jangle to the track,
Mom said no, but who's holding the snack?

The tree leans left, wisdom it lacks,
As holiday cheer fills the cracks.
Time for a nap? Oh, not yet dear,
The fun's just starting, bring on the cheer!

Echoes of Laughter in the Chill

Snowflakes flutter, soft and light,
While cousins argue over a snowball fight.
Frosty's hat flies, it's really quite sad,
And Grandpa slips—oh, isn't that bad?

We build a snowman with a huge grin,
But his carrot nose? We can't find where it's been.
Laughter echoes, crisp and clear,
Mom's hot cocoa, the best part of the year.

Sledding downhill, we rush with glee,
Tumble and roll, who fell? We all agree!
The chill nips at our nose, it seems,
Yet all we have are cozy daydreams.

Giggling echoes in the frosty air,
As friends and family dance without a care.
Sweaters too tight, but spirits take flight,
In this chilly wonderland, everything feels right!

Glistening Moments and Cozy Corners

In the corner, the dog stares wide,
At the glittering tree, where secrets hide.
Mom's first eggnog? It's gone to her head,
She danced on the table, what a thing she said!

Fireside chuckles, comfy and warm,
Dad's telling stories, passing the charm.
S'mores forgotten, chocolate in hand,
As grandma laughs, "No, he couldn't, he planned!"

Knitted socks with colors so bold,
Are starting to show their age as we're told.
Twinkling lights are the fairy dust,
Mom's ranting about cleaning? Well, no one must!

Warm memories drift on this cozy night,
In a house full of laughter, everything's right.
With the clock ticking down, and surprises so near,
These moments of joy are what we hold dear!

Surprises Tucked in the Hearth

Hiding gifts near the warm fireplace,
A sneaker, a sweater, oh what a place!
Sneaky peekers, trying their best,
To find out what's hidden, it's quite the quest.

The kettle whistles, loud and clear,
Hot apple cider, come gather here!
A secret ingredient? Just not a clue,
If anyone finds it, it would be you!

Jokes traded swiftly, between cookies and pie,
Great-aunt Sally's hat? My, what a style!
Smiles exchanged over games we play,
In this hearth of laughter, we welcome the day.

Laughter's the spice, joy's the key,
As we wrap up this holiday spree.
With surprises around every curve, it's true,
There's no place like home when shared with you!

Magic Beneath the Twilight Sky

In the glow of twinkling lights,
Where snowmen dance with pure delight.
Reindeer jumping, full of cheer,
Hope they don't trip on their own rear.

Cookies hide on every shelf,
Santa's sneaking, but what's that smell?
Is it burnt pie or sizzling ham?
Oh dear, I've gone and baked a spam!

Children giggle, chasing snow,
While Frosty shuffles, feeling slow.
Snowball fights break the calm,
Time to toss one at Aunt Pam!

Laughter echoes through the night,
As neighbors join in the snowball fight.
Under stars, our spirits soar,
Who knew winter held such galore?

Sugarplum Reveries

Dancing fairies in my dreams,
With jelly beans and chocolate streams.
Oh what fun it is to see,
Candy canes grow from the tree!

Marshmallow clouds float up so high,
Lollipop birds flit through the sky.
Who knew sugar could taste so grand?
I might just eat a whole candy band!

Chocolate rivers flow like tide,
As gumdrop castles sit with pride.
Dreams of sweets fill every night,
Might just get a sugar fright!

Jingle bells ring, oh so sweet,
A gingerbread man jumps to his feet.
Wishing for treats, oh what's the fuss?
Maybe just grab another bus!

Celebrations in the Air

Balloons bouncing, oh what fun,
Confetti flies, we've just begun!
Party hats and silly tunes,
Me and a bunch of dancing loons.

Cupcakes stacked like little towers,
Bring them forth, the sugary powers!
But wait, who dropped the chocolate cake?
Looks like more mess than a mistake!

Streamers hanging, blowing around,
We lose our snacks, they hit the ground.
Grab a plate or risk the fall,
Birthday cheers, let's have a ball!

Fireworks pop, colors burst bright,
Squirrels steal snacks—they think it's a fright!
The best of times, friends everywhere,
Raising a glass, let's all declare!

Misty Nights

Misty evenings under the glow,
Where secrets dance in the winter snow.
Ghosts in flannel, oh what a sight,
Cackling loudly, holding on tight.

Whispers float like fog on high,
A cat in slippers, oh my, oh my!
Chasing shadows, making a fuss,
We all scream, who's making that fuss?

Ghostly figures make their way,
Through fields where screeching owls play.
Holding hands through the eerie scene,
Hoping to wake from this wild dream!

In laughter, we find warmth and glee,
As shadows dance, just you and me.
The night unfolds, what will it bring?
Let's all pretend we're just bling-bling!

Warm Hearts

In a cozy nook with friends so dear,
Sipping cocoa, full of cheer.
With marshmallows floating like dreams,
We heap on love, bursting at the seams.

Fuzzy socks and mismatched shoes,
Playing games, singing the blues.
Cookies piled, oh what a sight,
Who knew sharing could start a fight?

Giggles echo, bright as the sun,
Warm embraces, oh what fun!
In this moment, all is well,
Like stories whispered from a shell.

As laughter fills this tiny space,
Creating memories time can't erase.
Hold your hearts close, let love ignite,
We'll share this warmth into the night!

Happiness in Every Bite

A cookie danced on the table,
It slipped and fell with a crunch.
Sugar sprinkles flew like confetti,
As I quickly made my lunch.

The cake sang a merry song,
While pie tried to steal the show.
Whipped cream was a splashy diva,
And I laughed, oh how I know!

Brownies wrestled with the pudding,
Each claiming the title of best.
In this sweet battle of flavors,
My taste buds won the grand fest!

So let's raise a glass of cocoa,
To desserts that bring such cheer,
As delight fills every corner,
With each bite, smiles appear!

Glittering Wishes on Snowy Eves

Snowflakes danced in the moonlight,
While snowmen strutted with glee.
Their carrot noses a bit crooked,
But who would dare disagree?

The reindeer took a wrong turn,
And ended up near the tree.
They nibbled on some tinsel,
Saying, 'Is that meant for me?'

Ornaments giggled with laughter,
As they hung on branches bare.
A star winked at the snowmen,
With an icy, mischievous flair.

On this night of snowy magic,
Silly wishes float around.
With each twinkle and giggle,
Joy in the air can be found!

Heartfelt Gatherings

Grandma's kitchen smells like magic,
With sauces brewing and beads.
The dog steals a slice of turkey,
While everyone laughs and feeds.

Uncle Joe told his wild stories,
Of fishing trips that went wrong.
Fish that got away, he claims,
In a performance that's quite strong.

Cousins built a tower of cookies,
That toppled like a clumsy tower.
Sprinkles rained like confetti,
And they laughed for half an hour.

In these moments full of laughter,
And warmth that fills the room,
Heartfelt gatherings remind us,
Of love's ever-blooming bloom!

Whirlwind of Joyful Memories

The holiday lights twinkled wildly,
As the cat chased after a ball.
It pounced with such fierce determination,
And crashed into the wall!

Silly games filled the evening,
With laughter echoing bright.
A family dance-off erupted,
In the glow of the fairy light.

Wrapping gifts became a circus,
With ribbons flying askew.
"Is this for me?" a voice questioned,
As the puppy pranced into view.

These chaotic moments we treasure,
With a smile and a cheer so loud.
Each whirlwind of joyful memory,
Plants our hearts in festive proud!

Dreams Dancing in Frosty Air

In a wintery whirl, we skip and twirl,
Chasing snowflakes that swirls and swirls.
With frosty breath, we make a laugh,
Building snowmen, our chilly craft.

Hot cocoa spills, but we don't care,
We toast to friends in the frosty air.
Snowball fights and silly grins,
This silly dance is where it begins.

With mittens paired and noses bright,
We grace this winter's evening light.
Giggles echo, escape the chill,
These frosty nights, they surely thrill.

Candy-Kissed Twilight and Glimmering Nights

With candy canes in our hands all night,
We jingle bells and take to flight.
Twinkling lights on houses gleam,
As we polish off our sugar cream.

The gingerbread men start to frown,
As we munch our way right through the town.
Marshmallows bouncing, giggles thus,
In candy castles, we make a fuss.

The cocoa's hot, the laughter pure,
Come join the fun! We're here for sure.
So grab a friend, don't you be shy,
Let's make it sweet as we fly high!

Laughter Hanging from the Roof

As snowflakes fall, we laugh aloud,
Tickling each other, we're quite the crowd.
Stockings hung with such flair and fun,
We'll see whose gift outshines the sun.

The cat's in a hat, what a sight to see,
She swats at baubles, how silly is she!
'Tis a season for mischief, let's not forget,
As we dance and twirl with glee and fret.

Our jingle bells clatter on the floor,
Step on the cat? Oh, what a score!
With laughter ringing from the roof,
It's a comical season, that's the truth!

Glow of Candles and Heartfelt Hugs

The candles flicker with a warm embrace,
As we gather 'round this silly space.
With heartfelt hugs and playful jests,
We share our wishes, we're truly blessed.

In each twinkling flame, a tale unfolds,
Of mishaps, laughter, and joys of old.
Our holiday punch, it's splashed and spilled,
But the merriment here, it cannot be killed.

With every chuckle, the night grows bright,
As we sing carols, not quite alright.
Through hugs and giggles, we hold on tight,
Spreading joy on this wondrous night!

Starlit Paths to Hidden Joy

Under twinkling skies we roam,
Chasing giggles, feeling home.
Snowflakes dance, they spin and twirl,
As laughter wraps around the world.

With every step, a joke blooms bright,
Sledding sideways, what a sight!
Hot cocoa spills, we share our treats,
Chocolate smudges on our cheeks.

A snowman's hat falls off his head,
He wobbles, laughs, then rolls instead.
Each chilly breeze whispers a tease,
In this winter, we're all at ease.

So grab your scarf, don't overthink,
Let's sip on cheer, and laugh, and wink.
Life's a funny, frosty spree,
With all our friends, it's joy for free!

Whispers of Frost on the Windowpane

Frosty patterns on my glass,
Like kittens prancing on the grass.
I sip my tea, it spills on me,
A winter clumsiness, oh, what glee!

Snowflakes drop in playful cheer,
A bird sneezes, oh dear, oh dear!
We build a fort that's never done,
It collapses first, oh what fun!

With mittens mismatched, we head outside,
To catch snowballs, nowhere to hide.
Slipping here and sliding there,
Who knew winter could be so rare?

Back inside, we'll warm our toes,
And laugh at how it all just goes.
Underneath the chilly moon,
Our silly spirits break into tune!

Gathering Shadows and Shimmering Recollections

In the twilight, shadows play,
Whispering secrets of the day.
In the corner, cookies stare,
We nibble lightly, oh, beware!

A cat leaps, knocking over treats,
We're redecorating with our feats.
Laughter echoes, the night is young,
Each silly tale is deftly spun.

The tree lights flicker, half a fight,
As garlands tangle, holding tight.
We'll string them up with all our might,
And giggles will fill the starlit night.

So gather close, let stories flow,
Each memory is a luminous glow.
In this whirligig of joy and play,
We find our mirth in the light of the day!

Soft Raindrops of Silver Tinsel

Silver threads hang from the eaves,
A sparkling touch, oh how it weaves.
Rain drips down, it's not quite snow,
Who needs a coat, just let it flow!

Tinsel falls like confetti bright,
As we dance in this glimmering light.
Umbrellas flipped, we splash through muck,
These silly days bring us pure luck.

Each puddle's a mirror, we sing aloud,
Wishing we were lost in the crowd.
Snowmen giggle, their noses bright,
In this wonder, we take flight.

So here's to mirth in every drop,
To joyful tunes that never stop.
In this season of playful schemes,
We wrap our hearts in silly dreams!

Bottled Wishes in the Night

In a bottle, I sent my cheer,
Hoping the neighbors wouldn't hear.
A cork popped loud, the fizz took flight,
They found it bouncing in the night.

Found my wishes under the tree,
Wishing for cookies, not just tea.
The reindeer laughed as they flew by,
Eating my cupcakes, oh my, oh my!

Santa's sleigh stuck in a shrub,
He called for help, but who to grub?
The elves just sat and sipped their punch,
With gingerbread men, they had a lunch.

So come dance in your festive shoes,
With jellybean colors, pick your blues.
And when you wish upon a star,
Make sure to aim your dreams afar.

Hugs and Hot Cocoa

Hot cocoa spills on my fluffy socks,
Chocolate kisses, we'll use them as clocks.
A tick-tock laughs from the chocolate mug,
Sipping giggles, all snug as a bug.

Baked cookies shaped like our cat,
He sniffed the air and said, "What's that?"
We chased him off, the dough was warm,
But then the dog showed up—a different charm!

Tiny marshmallows falling like snow,
In our mugs they start to flow.
A plop and a fizz, hear the joy rise,
Watching hot cocoa become a surprise!

Oh, sipping sweetness by the fire,
With laughter that never seems to tire.
Hugs fill the room, like fluff on a cloud,
Together, we sing and laugh out loud!

Christmas Lights and Silent Nights

The lights are tangled, a holiday sight,
They sparkled like stars, oh what a fright!
But in the jumble, I slipped and fell,
Now the dog thinks I'm part of the bell.

Silent nights turned into silly fights,
With snowballs tossed and pillow delights.
The ornaments giggled, as we tried to sneak,
A sneaky snack break for the cheeky peak.

Tree-top star doing the funky dance,
We hesitate, take a second glance.
Tinsel everywhere, it's a shiny mess,
But who could care? It's all about zest!

A chorus of laughter, the merry cheer,
With quirky carols, we spread good cheer.
So come, join the fun, put on a smile,
And twirl in the magic for a little while!

Boughs Heavy with Cheer

Boughs of joy hang low on the ground,
With cookies and laughter, we gather 'round.
The cats climb high, on branches they sway,
While we sing tunes that had gone astray.

Gingerbread houses not quite so neat,
With candy cane fences, they're still a treat.
But when the dog jumps, it all goes a'plop,
We laugh till we snort and can't even stop!

On snowy nights wrapped snug and tight,
Our sparkling dreams take thrilling flight.
With laughter that echoes through the chilled air,
Every crazy moment, a memory rare.

So deck the halls with giggles galore,
And sprinkle holiday cheer from door to door.
Let's twirl and leap till the dawn breaks clear,
With every silly wish, bringing us near!

Resplendent Baubles and Festive Cheer

Sparkles dance on every tree,
As cat pulls down the tinsel spree.
Unwrap the gifts with glee and fright,
Did Grandma send that crazy light?

Gingerbread men with frosting smiles,
Making mischief all the while.
Kids giggle and parents sigh,
As ornaments go flying high!

A hat made of a turkey cloth,
What's this? A gift that's just a sloth!
Dancing with a sock on each hand,
Creating chaos that's simply grand!

Laughter rings o'er cups of cheer,
As auntie serves the fruitcake here.
Unusual treats and games that tease,
Holiday fun that's sure to please!

Evergreen Adventures

Bundled up in scarves so bright,
Out we go, oh what a sight!
Sledding down a snowy hill,
With laughter echoing, what a thrill!

Snowflakes stick on noses round,
Someone's face is stuck in mounds!
Building snowmen, eyes of coal,
Carrot noses make them whole.

Hot cocoa spills on brand new clothes,
Mom just gasps, but the fun just grows.
A snowball fight turns to a scheme,
Revenge is sweet, or so we dream!

As evening falls, the stars come out,
A holiday dance brought a shout.
With two left feet, we stomp and prance,
In our hearts, we twirl, we dance!

Echoes of Holiday Laughter

Echoes of joy fill every room,
As uncle Fred starts to consume.
Holiday hats that light up red,
Are definitely on his head!

A game of charades gone quite awry,
Grandpa impersonates a fly!
With flapping arms and squeaky voice,
A family mess, oh what a choice!

Tickling kids while cookies bake,
Watch your fingers, for goodness' sake!
Dancing crumbs with every cheer,
A flour storm begins to clear!

When day turns night, the lights aglow,
We gather round to swap the show.
With cheeks aglow and hearts so light,
We celebrate, 'til the morning light!

Sweet Treats at Twilight

Candies piled both high and wide,
Chocolate rivers, we can't abide!
Sticky fingers, a gooey fate,
Sampling sweets, oh how we rate!

Taffy pulls and caramel falls,
Sugar high—a few late calls!
Cookies shaped like funny bears,
Tummies rumble, oh who dares?

Twirl around the candy cane,
Silly games bring joy and pain!
As fog descends, we laugh and sing,
Magical moments that winter brings.

With marshmallow fluff on our noses,
Holiday spirit—who supposes?
We clink our mugs, let joy resound,
In sugary bliss, we are unbound!

Enchanted Nights and Cozy Delights

Under twinkling lights so bright,
A snowman sneezes in sheer fright.
Hot cocoa spills from my mug,
As I trip on a dog's snug rug.

Laughter echoes in the air,
As Uncle Joe loses his chair.
The cat leaps over grandma's hat,
And juggles all of our leftovers flat.

With marshmallow snowballs we play,
As Auntie's wig goes astray.
Each giggle adds to the mirth,
While we revel in this warm hearth.

The fireplace crackles with cheer,
While grandpa tells tales we hold dear.
In this bubble of joy and glee,
We raise our mugs, let's all agree!

Savoring the Chill

Frosty air nips at my nose,
I dance in boots, strike a pose.
Snowballs fly and laughter roars,
Until someone knocks on the doors.

Sledding down the hill with glee,
Oh no, there goes my cup of tea!
With chilly fingers, we make a wish,
For hot soup served in a big dish.

The flakes blanket ground so white,
But I'm falling flat, what a sight!
With cheeks as red as a cherry pie,
This winter fun makes spirits fly.

We gather round with silly hats,
And we play games with our fat cats.
As we sip on drinks with a grin,
May this frosty joy never thin!

Where Snowflakes Dance

Snowflakes whirl like a waltzing crew,
While I try to catch one or two.
But my tongue gets stuck on a pole—
A winter tale that's out of control.

The sleigh bells jingle with delight,
As we slide past a snowman in flight.
Oh dear, Aunt Elsie's hat goes flying,
While we all burst out squealing, crying.

We build a fort, oh what a sight,
With snow bricks stacked high, it's a fight!
Snowballs soar like missiles of cheer,
As we laugh until we shed a tear.

Later we feast on cookies galore,
While munching and chatting, we want more!
With laughter echoing through the night,
These whimsical times feel just right.

The Glow of Hearth and Home

In cozy corners, we gather tight,
With fuzzy socks, a warming sight.
Stories shared by the fire so bright,
While shadows dance, our hearts take flight.

A cat with dreams of a roast,
Sits near the flames as we all boast.
Yet the turkey's escaped from the pan,
What a mess—oh! Who's the man?

Hiccups and giggles fill the air,
As we bake in fun without a care.
Grandma's secret, oh maybe not,
Who knew the cookies would taste so hot?

With plates piled high, we raise a cheer,
As we toast to friends, both far and near.
These moments, wrapped in laughter's embrace,
Fill our hearts, our favorite place.

Flickering Lights and Wishes Untold

In a tangle of lights, my thought runs,
Scaring the cat, while I chase for fun.
Cookies are burning, the timer didn't ring,
Swirling around, what chaos will bring?

Laughter erupts with the mishaps and spills,
Eggnog poured high gives everyone thrills.
Grandma's nog's potent, we sing off-key,
Dance with the tree – it's a sight to see!

A reindeer costume, worn with such pride,
Tripping on tinsel, it's quite the ride.
In this wild mess, we find festive cheer,
Who knew holiday madness could draw us near?

So raise up your glasses, let's toast to our blunders,
Through giggles and snorts, our joy just thunders.
With flickering lights, let the stories unfold,
In the warmth of our laughter, let love take hold.

Silent Nights and Bundled Dreams

Beneath the starlight, bundled up tight,
I lost my mitten, oh what a sight!
Snowflakes are falling, landing on noses,
Chasing winter rabbits, giving them poses.

A snowman contest, my carrot's a joke,
His smile's a grin, did he just poke?
Fingers are frozen, lips turning blue,
What do you mean, it's sleighing, not glue?

Hot cocoa spills down my front, what a mess!
Who knew it was space that I'd have to impress?
But with friends all around, and laughter so near,
Even the frosty bites disappear.

So here's to the nights under blankets so deep,
With snorts and warm blankets, we giggle and sleep.
In the chill of the season, we find cozy schemes,
Silent, yet bursting with frosty dreams.

Winter's Sweet Embrace

The wind's a comedian, tickling our cheeks,
Sidewalks are icy, I'm doing the tweaks.
Fluffy white snow, oh what a disguise,
I tripped on a sled; that's my Christmas surprise!

In woolly socks, I slip and I slide,
Wishing my balance was on my side.
Winter's a prankster, it pushes and shoves,
But we'll hold onto each other, that's how winter loves.

So gather your buddies for snowball fights,
Dodging the frost with giggles and bites.
Laughter erupts with each snowy fling,
In this icy embrace, joy is king!

With mugs full of cheer and love's warm embrace,
We dance in the snow, what a magical place.
Through frosty mishaps and smiles so bright,
Winter's embrace is pure delight.

Frosted Hopes and Dreaming Hearts

Under twinkling stars, we gather tonight,
With frosted hopes, everything feels right.
Grandma's old quilt wraps us up tight,
We giggle and dream until morning light.

In the kitchen, disasters await,
Burnt cookies and laughter are on our plate.
Sugar high children run wild and free,
Oops! That was icing, not meant for. . . me!

Snow forts and battles, a clash of pure fun,
Dodging and diving, oh how we run!
With every cold splash, our joy multiplies,
Seeing the world through bright, laughing eyes.

So here's to the season of frosty delight,
Where hopes come alive in the chill of the night.
With dreaming hearts, let our laughter echo,
In this winter wonderland, our spirits will glow.

Icy Paths and Warming Smiles

Through icy paths we laugh and slide,
Falling over, with arms open wide.
A snowball flies, what's the score?
We're giggling loudly, wanting more!

The frostbite nips, but hearts stay light,
Our rosy cheeks, a comical sight.
Hot cocoa spills in our wild play,
Who knew winter could bring such sway?

We dance around in scarves so bright,
Trip over boots in joyful fright.
Laughter echoes through the chill,
Especially when we trip down a hill!

So grab a friend, let's make some cheer,
Forget the cold, we bring the heat here!
With warming smiles we fight the frost,
In icy paths, we never get lost!

Unwrapping Joy

With wrapping paper flying around,
We tear through gifts without a sound.
What's inside? A rubber duck!
Oh wait, that's just my special luck!

Tinsel strands caught in our hair,
Making us look like we just don't care.
A gift of joy, a joke or two,
Who wrapped a lump of stinky goo?

Each box reveals a silly surprise,
Like socks that glow and big fake eyes.
We laugh and dance in messy flair,
Remarkable gifts that we all can share!

So let's unwrap the love we see,
In moments shared so joyfully.
From strange to sweet, what a delight,
Unwrapping joy through day and night!

Cookies and Kindness

In the kitchen, the chaos reigns,
Flour flying like it's in our veins.
Cookies baking, the sweet scent calls,
But someone tripped and down went all!

Mixing bowls go clatter, smash,
While everyone scrambles, oh what a crash!
Sugar spills like a snowstorm's might,
Leaving us giggling through the night!

With sprinkles and frosting, we decorate,
But someone's kitty just can't wait!
A swipe and a paw, oh what a sight,
Our kitchen now a chaotic fright!

Yet kindness lingers in every bite,
As cookies shared bring pure delight.
Through laughter and crumbs, friendships bind,
In cookies and kindness, joy we find!

Hopes Adrift on Cold Breezes

As cold winds blow, we play and spin,
Hopes drift by like a lost paper bin.
Each wish we cast, a kite in the sky,
With giggles that flutter, oh me, oh my!

Snowflakes dance with winks and grace,
Like winter confetti at our place.
Chasing dreams, we run and whirl,
While scarves get tangled, our heads in a twirl!

Sipping warm drinks while breaths turn to mist,
In slow motion, joy that can't be missed.
Hopes afloat like feathers in flight,
With each laugh, we soar through the night!

So let's share dreams on these frigid thrills,
In this cold, warmth flows with mighty spills.
With every chuckle, let worries freeze,
As we ride the wind, like hopes on the breeze!

The Sweetness of Togetherness

Gather 'round, it's time to cheer,
With cookies, giggles, and a pint of beer.
Laughter echoes through the hall,
As Uncle Joe attempts a crawl.

The cat's adorned with tinsel bright,
While grandpa snags the last delight.
In every corner, joy's a must,
Even if the turkey's just a bust.

Plan a dance, or a silly game,
Who knew holiday cheer brought such fame?
A toast to friends, a toast to pie,
May our hearts soar, and spirits fly!

So raise a glass to silly feats,
And singing loud with off-key beats.
The sweet delight of all our kin,
This holiday fun, let's dive right in!

Frosty Air and Kindred Spirits

Bundle up, it's time for frost,
But don't you dare forget the cost.
Bring cocoa mugs, let's sip and spill,
While laughter dances up the hill.

Snowflakes fall on noses bright,
As snowmen take their clumsy flight.
With scarves and hats that don't quite match,
We'll craft a brother-sister batch!

Snowball fights turn into hugs,
While hot chocolate flows as snug.
In this chill, our spirits rise,
Kindred hearts are the greatest prize!

So grab a friend, and start a cheer,
Let merriment draw us near.
With frosty air and playful spark,
Our joy ignites the winter dark!

Yule's Guiding Glow

Lights aglow upon the tree,
A sight that brings such glee.
With ornaments that squeak and shine,
We'll laugh and sip our sweetened wine.

Silly hats and matching socks,
While doorbells ring in flurry knocks.
A family dance? Let's give it a whirl,
With twirls and twinkles as we swirl!

Old tales told in joyous jest,
Uncle's stories are the very best.
In the warmth of cheer we gather round,
With love and laughter all around.

Under the glow, we'll dream and play,
In the coziest of holiday way.
Our hearts, like candles, brightly beam,
As we create our festive dream!

Radiance Amidst the Snowfall

Snowflakes swirl like playful kids,
As laughter spills, we're all outdid.
With mugs held high and spirits so light,
Let's dance 'til the morning bright!

The raccoon's raided yet again,
He took our snacks—oh what a men!
But we can't fret with such delight,
As carols fill this snowy night.

Stockings hung with crafty care,
What's in there? Just winter fare.
With socks and trinkets, oh so keen,
The funniest gifts we've ever seen!

So here's to joy in every square,
With twinkling lights and love to share.
Amidst the snow, our hearts will glow,
With giggles soft, we steal the show!

Celestial Joys and Cinnamon Air

Under twinkling lights, we sing loud,
The cat's in the tree, oh so proud.
Ornaments dance, the cookies are gone,
Who knew that the elf was a sneaky con?

Snowmen wobble with carrots askew,
Their button eyes hide a laugh or two.
We throw snowballs with giggles and shouts,
Friends turn to snowflakes as snowflakes flout.

A reindeer prances, a jolly old spry,
Wearing a scarf, oh my, oh my!
With marshmallows floating in cocoa delight,
We're the goofy crew, what a silly sight!

So lift up your mugs, let laughter abide,
In this frosty wonder, let joy be our guide.
With cinnamon swirls and a side of cheer,
We'll dance through the season, year after year.

Dreams Wrapped in Woolen Scarves

Snuggled up tight in layers galore,
Finding lost mittens from last year's store.
Hot cocoa spills, oh what a delight,
Here comes the dog, ready for a bite!

With scarves on our heads and hats askew,
We stumble outside, just me and you.
We're now snowmen, who let it snow,
Twirling around, we're the stars of the show!

The snowball fight breaks out, oh what fun,
With laughter that bubbles like hot, spicy rum.
We fall in the fluff, making snow angels wide,
In a land of giggles, we take it in stride.

Each snowy jaunt fills our hearts with bliss,
Every tumble and shout, we simply can't miss.
As we wrap ourselves warm, giggles fill the air,
In our woolen cocoon, without a single care!

Sipping Joy from Mugs of Warmth

Mugs filled with magic, marshmallows afloat,
Giggling while we hold our hot chocolate boat.
Each sip is a potion of giggles and cheer,
Who knew joy could bubble with each tasty smear?

In fuzzy slippers, we dance on the floor,
While cookies beg us to munch and explore.
Chocolate chips fall like snowflakes of fun,
We munch and we crunch 'til the raiding is done!

As the kettle whistles with songs of delight,
We pour out the warmth that's cozy and bright.
Add in some sprinkles, a dollop of cream,
Dive into laughter, it's all just a dream!

So raise up your mugs, let our laughter ignite,
On this silly adventure, let's hold on so tight.
With joy in our hearts and smiles, not a scorn,
We sip on this magic, together reborn!

Frosty Footprints and Gleeful Hearts

In a world painted white, we leave our trace,
Tiny snowflakes tickle, we giggle with grace.
Frosty footprints dance, zigzagging in glee,
Each step a new riddle, who could it be?

The icicles dangle, a chandelier bright,
We pretend to be kings in the soft winter light.
With cheeks rosy red from the nippy parade,
Who would have thought that fun gets repaid?

Snow shovels are toys, and sleds take us far,
We soar down the hills, like a shooting star.
Then we tumble and roll, laughter fills the air,
In the frosty realm, everyone's a millionaire!

So let's chase the snowflakes and shout a loud cheer,
In the gleeful adventure, there's no room for fear.
With hearts full of humor and footprints in play,
This whimsical journey is the best kind of day!

Garland of Dreams

A ribbon wrapped 'round a gingerbread guy,
With frosting so bright, he's ready to fly.
He dances with joy, all twirls and spins,
While cats plot and scheme, for sugar-filled wins.

Tinsel on trees like a squirrel's wild hair,
Twinkling and giggling, causing a scare.
The lights are a-chase, like shadowy thieves,
As we laugh at the chaos, this season believes.

Jingle bells jangle, but what do they mean?
Is it joy or a call from the neighbor's machine?
We toast with hot cocoa, marshmallows afloat,
While visions of chaos sail past in a boat.

So bring on the laughter, the cookies, the cheer,
With each silly moment, we hold so dear.
The garland we weave is with laughter and dreams,
As we dance through the mayhem, or so it seems.

Comfort in the Chill

The snowflakes are landing, a fluffy white plume,
But it's not a soft bed, just a shivering room.
With hot cocoa flinging, I sip with a sigh,
As marshmallows leap, and my eyebrows go high.

The mittens are mismatched, a zebra with stripes,
While socks waltz together, defying all types.
We bubble and giggle, in warm, cuddly clothes,
As we plot our escape from the cold, winter woes.

The squirrels are feasting on acorns and pies,
While we huddle together, brewing our lies.
A snowman is watching, but he's frozen in glee,
With a carrot for laughter, and no sense of spree.

So gather your friends, forget all the chill,
With laughter and cookies, oh, what a thrill!
The warmth of our hearts will melt any frost,
Embrace every moment, and forget what was lost.

Lullabies of Frost and Fire

The fire crackles, pops like a fun little tune,
While frost waltzes in, like a mischievous balloon.
We cuddle up tight, with our snacks piled high,
As the marshmallows giggle, and shadows comply.

The holiday lights toss a glow on the wall,
Like a dance party thrown for a very odd ball.
With tinsel on heads, we declare, 'We're the kings!'
While laughing at the sound of our very own sings.

The cookies are baking, but wait, what a fright!
I'll bet they're rebelling, plotting all night.
With frosting like rain on a cookie parade,
We chat with each other, like we've all been made.

So raise up a glass to the frosty delight,
To fireside comforts, in giggles so bright.
With lullabies sung in the warmth of our home,
We'll dance through the night, with our wishes to roam.

Cinnamon Dreams by Candlelight

The scent of sweet cinnamon lingers and swirls,
As we sip on our drinks, letting laughter unfurl.
With candles that flicker, and frosting that gleams,
Let's dance with the shadows of our silly dreams.

The reindeer are plotting a holiday heist,
While cookies in cupboards are calling, "Be nice!"
We munch and we giggle, making quite a mess,
As cocoa spills over, oh, who'd ever guess?

The stockings are hung, with care and with flair,
But oh the surprise when we find that they're bare!
In a world of bright sprinkles and laughter galore,
Each moment we capture, we joyfully score.

So light up the candles and toast to delight,
To friends who are silly and hold our hearts tight.
With cinnamon memories and dreams that take flight,
We'll laugh through the night, sharing joy ever bright.

Time for Togetherness

Gather 'round, we're here again,
With cookies, laughter, and a friend.
A cat in a hat, a dog on a chair,
Who knew the holiday could bring such flair?

Hot cocoa splashes, oh what a sight,
As marshmallows float, oh what a delight!
Uncle Joe's jokes, they fly like a kite,
Just don't blame me if they don't land right!

Socks mismatched, oh what a thrill,
The family resemblance makes me chill.
But amidst all chaos, love is the key,
Even if Aunt Sue jumps into the tree!

So raise a toast, let's cheer it loud,
For all the mishaps that make us proud.
Let slip the puns, just like the cheer,
Until next year, we'll return right here!

Stories Shared by Firelight

By the crackling fire, stories abound,
The tall tales of Grandpa, oh how they crown!
With half-eaten pies and crumbs on his face,
He claims he once caught a fish in space!

Cousin Lou's antics will give you a chuckle,
When he tried to roast marshmallows, oh what a struggle.

His stick caught fire, how we all screamed,
But he just toasted, saying 'I dreamed!'

We pass the warm cider, and oh what a fuss,
The mug's got a chip, but we laugh with us.
In this joyful mess, we share every cheer,
Our hearts are like embers, glowing right here.

So gather those moments, hold them so tight,
For memories made are pure, pure delight.
With laughter and warmth, till the morning comes,
In the glow of our tales, love always hums!

Nostalgia Wrapped in Bow

Boxes of memories in ribbons galore,
Unwrapping the past, oh what a chore!
Old photos and letters, some quite bizarre,
Like Dad in a tutu, or Mom as a star!

That sweater from Auntie, scratchy and bright,
With buttons that jingle, it's quite a sight!
We'll laugh till we cry, as we recall,
The year that we almost forgot to install!

So let's raise a glass decorated with flair,
To nights filled with stories and silly despair.
With laughter as sprinkles on top of our pie,
We toast to the past, oh me, oh my!

In this cozy circle, wrapped in the glow,
The warmth of connection is all that we know.
Each moment a treasure, wrapped soft like a sigh,
With humor and love, the spirits fly high!

Chilled Air and Whispered Secrets

Under the stars, we whisper and schemes,
The frosty air filled with giggles and dreams.
Snowflakes fall gently, like small luck-filled hugs,
While secrets are shared 'neath the blankets and rugs.

In the chilly dark, with cheeks rosy red,
We plot the next prank for Uncle Fred.
But he snores so loud, it's hard to be sly,
Yet we can't help but laugh, oh my, oh my!

The snowman is lopsided, but who really cares?
With a carrot for a nose, he proudly stares!
As the cocoa warms hearts with giggles galore,
Even Mother Nature chuckles 'fore snore.

So let's dance in the shadows, throw caution to wind,
For each cozy moment, we happily rescind.
With chilled air and giggles, our spirits will soar,
Until next year's winter, let's create even more!

Magic Beneath the Stars

In the chilly night, we prance with glee,
Chasing shadows, who knows what they'll be?
Snowmen wobble, their noses askew,
With carrots misplaced, and eyes made of goo.

Elves have left cookies, treats galore,
But someone's been munching, oh what a chore!
Milk is a puddle, the cat's in a spin,
Next year, we'll hide it, let the chaos begin!

Shimmering Frost and Wistful Thoughts

The rooftops gleam with a ho ho ho,
While rooftops still echo a loud "whoa!"
Sleigh bells jingle, with rhythm so bright,
But Santa's sleigh got lost last night!

Carolers bust in, all out of tune,
A kitten joins in, it's quite the cartoon!
With laughter and giggles, our hearts take flight,
Who needs perfect when your cat sings right?

Gathered Around the Flame

Gathered 'round the fire, all wrapped up tight,
Some clash with chestnuts, a silly sight!
Hot cocoa spills, everyone squeals,
As marshmallows dance, defying all seals.

Uncles tell tales that get wilder each year,
Of treasure maps found, and dogs that steer!
With stories a-swirling, the laughter's a blast,
And grandma's recipe? We just hold our cast!

Secrets of the Winter Night

Under the moon, we dance with delight,
With mittens on paws, what a curious sight!
Snowflakes start falling, they tickle our nose,
As we twirl and tumble, everyone knows.

The stars whisper nonsense, each sparkle a pun,
We giggle and snicker, this night is just fun!
With wishes for spring, but here we stay,
Hoping the frost will just frolic away!

Glimmering Fir and Twinkling Dreamscapes

Under the twinkling lights so bright,
A tree's adorned in sheer delight.
Ornaments hang, some upside down,
A squirrel could wear that sparkly crown!

The tinsel behaves like a slithering snake,
A cat will pounce, oh for goodness' sake!
Gifts wrapped in paper, too shiny to last,
A tape monster's lurking, we're stuck to the past!

Hot cocoa spills, a marshmallow fight,
Who knew such joy could cause such a fright?
Snowflakes tumble like clumsy dancers,
We laugh so hard, they're trying their chances!

So here's to the cheer and laughter galore,
As we trip over socks, oh what a chore.
The holiday spirit, it tickles the heart,
With giggles and fun, we'll never part!

Guests of the Holiday Spirit

Uninvited guests, they come with flair,
Tiny elves dancing on kitchen chairs.
The cookies vanish, a sugary theft,
With crumbs and giggles, a little bit heft!

The dog wears a hat, quite proud of his role,
While the cat rolls her eyes, she plays the scroll.
Grandma's knit sweater, a bright neon glow,
She's the fashion icon, we all know!

Frosty the snowman, he melts with a grin,
Waving goodbye as the warmth creeps in.
But who can resist those hot treats around?
With laughter and love, pure joy can be found!

So, raise up your mugs to the mirth we've bred,
For all the surprises that dance in our head.
As we welcome the cheer with glasses held high,
With quirky traditions, we'll get by!

The Cozy Nest of Seasons

In a nook by the fire, we snuggle tight,
Blankets and laughter cozy up the night.
The cat's on the mantle, a prince in his spot,
Wishing for warmth, he's giving it a shot!

Outside the windows, the snowflakes tumble,
With each little flake, our laughter does rumble.
A snowman appears, all lopsided and blue,
Waving hello—what mischief we'll do!

Hot chocolate flows like a river of dreams,
With whipped cream mountains and marshmallow streams.
We'll sip and we'll chuckle, make silly small cheers,
While secretly wishing none of us steers!

So gather your friends near the glow of the fire,
With stories and giggles that never tire.
We wish for the joy that this season brings,
In our cozy nest where the laughter sings!

The Dance of Winter's Spirit

Snowflakes waltz like they know the move,
Tip-tap on rooftops, showing their groove.
The wind sings a tune, a cheeky ballet,
While squirrels take bets on the best nut buffet!

Ice skating shuffles, we stumble and fall,
Pretending it's graceful; we're having a ball.
With slippery sneakers and giggles that swell,
We'll laugh through the chaos, oh what a spell!

Winter's ball calls us, a bash out in white,
With hot cider to warm us; it feels just right.
A snowball fight breaks all doubt and despair,
As we freeze-time together, with friendship to share!

So put on your hat, let your spirit ignite,
In this Winter's dance, everything feels bright.
With memories formed in the frosty delight,
We twirl through the snow on this magical night!

Sweets of the Season

In a land where sugar plums all dance,
The reindeer prance with barely a chance.
Muffins sing carols, oh what a sight,
Cookies with frosting, all dressed up tight.

Gumdrops are jiving, the licorice spins,
Lollipops giggle, oh where do we begin?
Frothy hot cocoa with a splash of cheer,
Marshmallows toast by the fire, oh dear!

Fairies are baking, they keep it discreet,
But frosting's a challenge; it's hard to compete.
Chocolate chip chaos, it's sprinkle confetti,
I'm stuck on my couch, but my heart feels all ready.

So hoist up the fruitcake, give him a cheer,
While we nibble on snacks, oh holiday dear!
The laughter is sweet, like a candy parade,
In this dessert wonderland where dreams are made.

Dreams Beneath the Evergreen

Beneath the tall trees, where the squirrels play,
Jingle bells echo, just a hop away.
Dreams of hot cider, and blankets so warm,
But first, we must dodge a snowman alarm!

What's that in the air? Is it laughter or cream?
An elf with a tutu, is this just a dream?
A reindeer on roller skates, gliding around,
Hilarity strikes, as we tumble down!

The ornaments chuckle; they wink as they shine,
A candy cane choir sings, 'Everything's fine!'
With garlands of giggles and lights everywhere,
We dance through the snow, without a single care.

So let's embrace chaos, like whims in the wind,
With laughter and apples that twirl as they spin.
Under the stars that twinkle like gold,
This season's a circus, a sight to behold.

Candy Cane Whispers

Whispers of sugar, in the night so bright,
A gumdrop angel took off in flight.
Lollipops giggle, as they tap on the glass,
Sweets in the pantry plan mischief en masse.

Bows on the packages, ribbon so sly,
Who wrapped all the gifts? Oh my, oh my!
Crispy, crunchy snacks are causing a fuss,
My puppy's in trouble, oh, what a plus!

Sprinkles are bouncing, all over the floor,
While chocolate pretzels start jumping for more.
Fudge takes a tumble, he lands with a plop,
This kitchen's a circus, it's ready to pop!

So come join the fun, let's all join the cheer,
For giggles and snacks, let's start the New Year!
With laughter like frosting and joy like a scream,
We'll chase all the goofballs and live our sweet dream.

Frosty Night Serenade

On a night so frosty, with lights all aglow,
We hum silly carols while cookies throw dough.
Snowflakes are twirling, in a wild ballet,
And frosty the snowman starts crooning away.

The cat's in the tree, while the dog takes a peek,
He's eyeing the cookies, paws ready to sneak.
With tinsel and razzle, the whole house is stirred,
A candy cane chorus, oh what a big herd!

Marshmallows melt, in the cocoa so sweet,
But watch out for cocoa that's claiming a seat!
Chocolate unicorns whisk through the night,
Spreading joy and laughter, oh what a sight!

So toast to the madness, raise mugs filled with cheer,
For laughter and sweetness is why we are here.
Under stars that giggle, and snowflakes that play,
We'll dance through the night, in a merry ballet.

Enchanted Sprigs of Evergreen

Beneath the branches, I sneak a peek,
Finding a squirrel who's ready to speak.
He chats about berries and nuts for the feast,
While I can't stop laughing, it's comic at least.

With garlands of laughter, we frolic around,
Tickling the pinecones that tumble to ground.
The tree has the giggles, I swear it's alive,
As ornaments wiggle, the branches contrive.

A snowman looks grumpy, he's losing his hat,
Blaming the neighbors for all of that chat.
They're stealing his scarf, what a terrible crime,
But we all agree, it's just wintertime.

So let's raise a toast with some hot cocoa cheer,
To all the gnomes dancing; they bring so much weird.
With spruce-scented magic, this season is bright,
Laughing with friends makes the cold feel just right.

Cherished Moments Beneath the Stars

Gathering 'round, in our flannel pajamas,
We share tales of conquer and buttered bananas.
The stars are all winking; they know what we've done,
While marshmallows roast, we laugh 'til we're done.

A raccoon appears with a festive cap,
Stealing our cookies, oh dear, what a trap!
But with sprinkles of glitter, we craft a new plan,
To lure him with candy, that clever raccoon man.

Moments like these filled with giggles and glee,
Dance through our minds with a sprinkle of spree.
Under the blanket of twinkling lights,
We cherish this chaos, those wild, funny nights.

So here's to the laughter, the memories bright,
Of mishaps and banter by warm firelight.
We'll make some more stories, too fun to define,
With stars as our witnesses, everything's fine.

Tinsel Tales and Sparkling Echoes

In a world of tinsel, where bright colors swirl,
We made a fine mess with a laugh and a twirl.
Granny's old ornaments kept jumping with cheer,
As we danced 'round the tree with mischief and beer.

Uncle Bob turned up, in a costume so bright,
He startled the cat, what a comical fright!
With lights that kept blinking in awkward arrays,
Our dance turned to chaos—those were funny days.

A toast with our glasses, they clinked and they fell,
Spilling the punch—what a humorous spell.
Laughter erupted as we tried to clean,
With jelly-stained shirts, we looked quite the scene.

So here's to the stories that sparkle and gleam,
A celebration wrapped in a raucous dream.
With tinsel and giggles, we'll forever remain,
The joyous misfits of our festive domain.

Wishes Wrapped in Velvet Starlight

With soft velvet wishes tucked under our beds,
We hustle and bustle, all thoughts in our heads.
We dream of the snacks that will come out to play,
As glittering giggles brush sleepiness away.

Wrapped in twinkling lights, the cats supervise,
They claim all the ribbons and toys as their prize.
What's this? A cat scratch on my favorite star?
Well, midnight mischief just travelled too far!

So let's reminisce about silly old days,
When our socks vanished in mysterious ways.
The stockings all jumbled, quite riddled with cheer,
We laugh at the moments that bring us so near.

In cozy concoctions of friendship and fun,
We sip on hot chocolate 'til everything's done.
With wishes exchanged, laughter bright as the night,
These velvet wrapped dreams fill our hearts with delight.

Winter's Whispers and Candy Cane Hopes

Snowflakes tumble down, oh what a sight,
A snowman's carrot nose is wobbly, quite right!
Chasing after the dog, who steals my warm glove,
Hot cocoa in hand, I just can't get enough!

Elf on the shelf, he's been quite a tease,
Dancing on the mantel, he does as he please.
A candy cane forest grows taller each day,
Who knew sweet treats could giggle and play?

Sledding on hills that seem much too steep,
Hoping to land without making a heap.
My friend's hat is lost, blown off by the breeze,
Chasing it down, I trip over a freeze!

As winter days pass, let laughter be found,
With snowball fights broken by giggles around.
Here's to the moments, both goofy and bright,
In snowy adventures, we find our delight!

Sugarplum Secrets Unwrapped

Under the tree, a gift with a bow,
I shake it a bit, but what could it stow?
Is it socks or a toy, a cat with a hat?
I dare not open it, what if it's that?

The cookies are baked, but now they are gone,
The dog's left a trace, of sprinkles and dawn.
With chocolate-stained fingers, I try to conceal,
That I've eaten half of my sugar-filled meal!

Wrapping up gifts, oh what a great mess,
In ribbons and tags, I'm a total distress.
But then there is laughter, and music from cheer,
Who needs perfection when fun's in the air?

So here's to the secrets, the giggles they bring,
As we unwrap joy in a colorful fling.
With laughter and joy, let the stories unfold,
In the season of sweets, let the fun be retold!

Frosted Nights and Joyful Lights

Frosted the windows, a glittering scene,
We're cozy inside, feeling festive and keen.
Lights twinkle brightly on the house down the lane,
Dogs bark with glee, trying hard to explain!

An igloo of ice, we built with such care,
Only to find that a raccoon is there.
He plunders the snacks that we change for a bite,
Was it really a party? It felt quite polite!

We hang up the stockings, stockings so wide,
What will be stuffed there? A cat could decide!
Toothbrushes, or candy? Oh what a grand find,
The wiggle of joy's in the air, intertwined!

So gather around, for the laughter in store,
With friends and some fun, there's always much more.
Let frosted nights bring us warmth and delight,
As we dance through this season, all merry and bright!

Holiday Breeze and Sweet Delights

A twinkle of lights on the neighborhood streets,
With cookies and songs, it's all just so sweet!
The caroling group sings off-key, that's for sure,
Yet laughter erupts, we couldn't ask for more.

Hot cider's a treat that spills on my shoe,
Carried by kids in a festive-hued crew.
They giggle and jump, their cheeks all aglow,
Chunky snowballs fly, and they put on a show!

With ribbons and bows spun from tape that won't quit,
I gift wrap my heart, it's the thought that is lit.
But somehow they end up tangled in fur,
It's the cat's little secret; oh, how she'd prefer!

So toast to the laughter that bubbles like cheer,
With each clink of glasses, we tighten the sphere.
For in this wild season, sweet moments arrive,
We dance through the chaos; it's jolly to thrive!